The New Yogi Manifesto

a collection of spiritual poems

with illustrations

The New Yogi Manifesto

by James Mihaley

Illustrated by Oshri Hakak

Published by Chariot of Kindness

First Edition
Copyright © 2015, by James Mihaley and Oshri Hakak
All Rights Reserved

The New Yogi Manifesto
Poetry by James Mihaley
Illustrations by Oshri Hakak

Published by Chariot of Kindness
Los Angeles
ISBN 978-0-692-44145-9

For Margaret Kelsey and James R. Mihaley. And for Gary and Elizabeth.

For Carole, Lev, Jacob, Rashelle, Tal, Elah, Noa, and Aiden.

For all yogis of all creeds, new and ancient.

Table of Contents

Invocation..2

The New Yogi Manifesto..................................4

A Fairy's Guide to Riding Roses.....................25

Man with a Toolbox.......................................28

The Break-In..32

Love Letter Written in Sears.........................33

Taiwan..35

Lady Who Rides a Bike..................................37

Monarchs..39

It Doesn't Get Much Better Than This..............56

Love Swept the Floor.....................................58

Yoga Ants..64

Scales..69

Finally I Can Relax..70

Love Thing..72

The Drought...83

Invocation

Do you see those chains lying on the floor,
the ones that used to bind you? Chains
you snapped in half through a simple act of
forgiveness. Chains you ripped from your heart
in order to feel more deeply. Chains called
sorrow and despair, rage and insincerity.
You peeled them off your essence and heaved
them into the pile. Somehow you picked the
lock on your own ego. You did it. It wasn't
your yoga teacher or your therapist or your
mother or your father. You did it by yourself,
in the middle of the night, with no one else
around, no one for miles, with your own bare
hands. Look at those chains on the floor.
A pile of chains.
Tell me you aren't brave.
Tell me you aren't powerful.
I dare you.

The New Yogi Manifesto

The new yogi believes that the word "Love"
has its own gong. The new yogi believes that
a shadow is not a shadow. It's a ray of light that's
taking a nap. The new yogi has a sign on her front
door that says: WARNING. I AM PRONE TO FITS
OF ANGELIC BEHAVIOR.

The new yogi is all colors, all genders, all ages,
5 years old, 35, 85, 105. If you own a yoga mat
and have ever sent a text message then you are a new
yogi. Deal with it. The new yogi gladly accepts her
destiny, to be incarnated in a frantic world.
She can handle it. The new yogi is tough.
Grace isn't fragile. She has trained for this.
Yoga is the ballet of the soul. Her
consciousness dances at the speed of light.

She is so calm yet so busy, so swift yet so still.
Her day is teeming yet tranquil.

Regardless of her hectic schedule, she floats
on the raft of her neutral mind down the
raging waters of rush hour, helping
people onto her raft, those drowning in fear,
resentment, alienation, pulling them onto her
raft while the crocodiles circle, peeling the
leeches off their arms and legs, the leeches of
a bankrupt culture that suck the grace out of
our bloodstream, tending to their wounds,
teaching them long deep breathing
on a raft floating through an intersection,
floating in the moonlight, a raft big enough for
half a dozen yoga mats, a raft lashed together
with bamboo, floating down the 21st century, a
woman on the raft of her neutral mind
teaching long deep breathing in the stillness.

She is employed by Love. Love hired her. Love interviewed her for the job in a tree house on a shooting star. Hers is a heart made out of yoga, a heart made out of yoga.

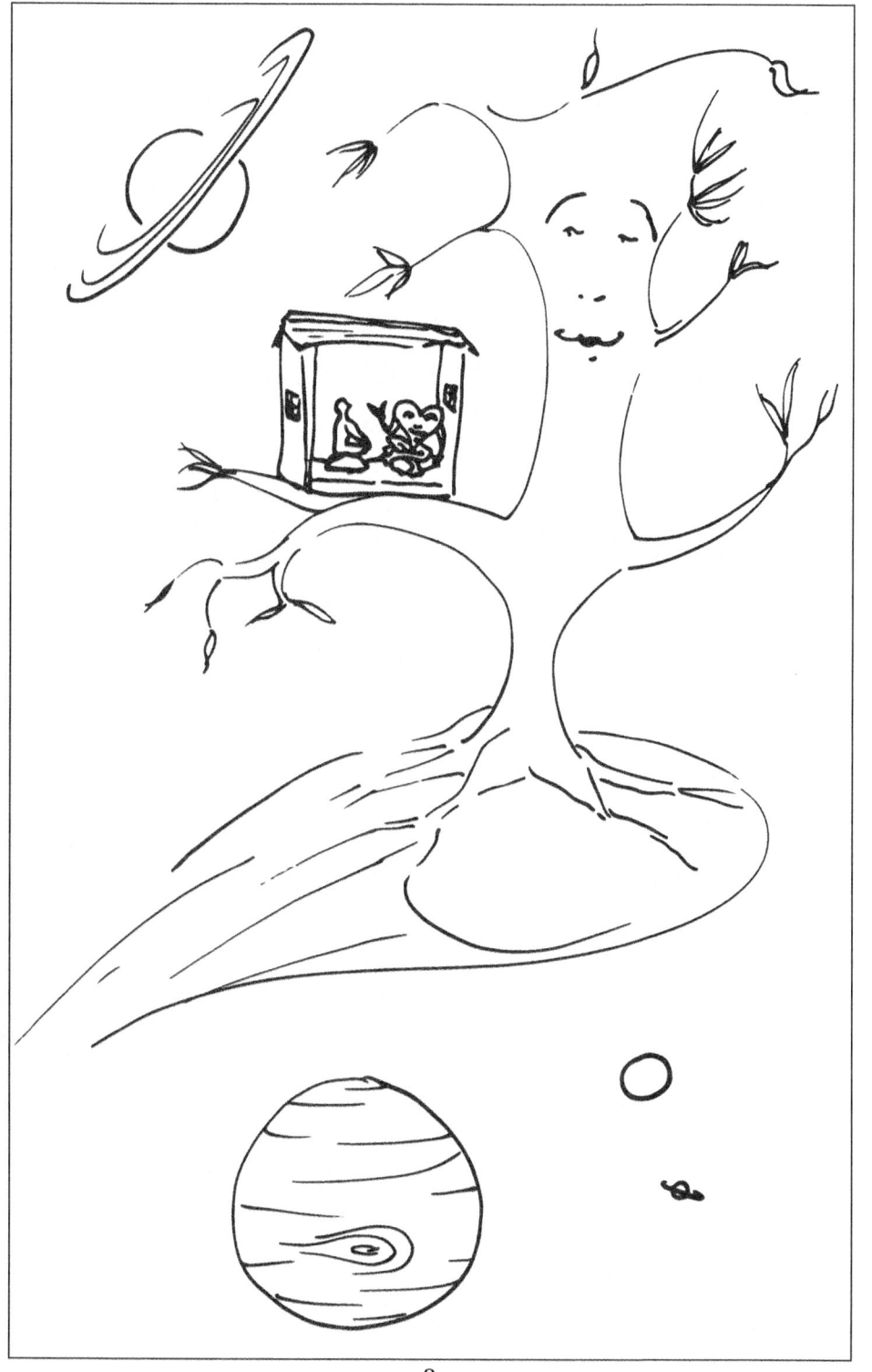

Despite all her attributes, you will not find the
new yogi on the cover of People magazine.
She will never get chased by paparazzi. She is
underground, way underground, building a
tunnel that connects all churches,

the only tunnel on Earth that is flooded with sunlight,
thousands of feet down and blazing with
golden light, the new yogi gripping a shovel,
surrounded by gophers and badgers and hedge
hogs who have come to help her dig, who
sense in her the spirit of the Great Earth Mother.

Because of her healing powers, the new yogi is not well liked by the pharmaceutical industry, whose motto is: THE ONLY PROBLEM WITH HAPPINESS IS THAT IT ISN'T MISERABLE. They plaster that message on their billboards.

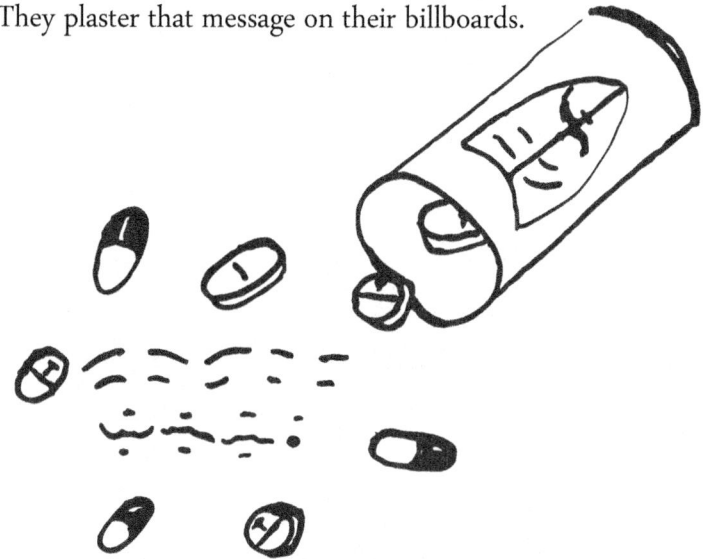

To counteract it, the new yogi created her own billboard with the help of her fellow yogis, through the power of group consciousness, an energetic billboard, an Aquarian billboard, and they placed it in a strategic location, where the 405 and the 10 intersect with the 837 and 958 and 335, all the highways of neurosis and greed and meanness, and the notorious 762, the superhighway of small thinking down which their speeds one million monkey minds, fifty lanes in each direction.

There at the intersection of all those roads,
at the precise point where all that madness
meets, without ever leaving their yoga mats,
they erected a towering billboard.
Undetectable to the five senses, it can only be
read by the soul,
and the billboard says:

When a friend asks the new yogi if it's possible to become an enlightened master even if you still owe money on your student loan, she says, "Hell yeah." The new yogi is busy giving good advice. She is busy being brave, busy evolving, busy forgiving herself, busy forgiving others, busy letting go, surrendering, so busy, so ultra-modern, so Oh my God, I can't believe it's four o'clock already, so busy she has to cancel her appointment with pettiness, her lunch date with envy and regret. She just can't fit them in anymore. She's too busy being grateful, busy being in a state of grace, a state of wonder.

So busy.

The To-Do list of the new yogi goes something like this:

1. Take son to soccer practice.
2. Levitate.
3. Buy quinoa and bran muffins.
4. Into the cooler of human consciousness add vibrational kombucha.
5. Buy sexy dress on sale at the mall.

The new yogi is busy laughing, never taking herself too seriously. What she does take seriously is the suffering of others. She is well aware that there was a mass shooting in Santa Barbara and the glaciers are melting and there's a drought going on. Prison populations are skyrocketing. So is the high school drop out rate. Corruption is rampant, drug abuse everywhere. On CNN experts spew out statistics to prove it.

To the Mass Media the new yogi says, "I hear your eloquent argument of despair but I am not convinced. I do not live in denial of these awful truths but I know that there is nothing in this world more powerful than a simple act of kindness. I will start there. I will start right there, rolling a burrito for a homeless man on Skid Row. One scoop of rice, two scoops of beans, three sprigs of cilantro. I carefully fold the tortilla so it doesn't tear. No one likes a leaky burrito. One step at a time, one burrito at a time, one breath at a time."

An hour later, she steps out of the food truck with a sack of burritos. In the gloom of downtown she wanders where rats scuttle. She understands that getting her hands dirty is the only way to get them clean.

The new yogi chants the phrase, "Free burritos, free burritos." A withered hand emerges from a slit inside a dirty tent and snatches a burrito. A minute later, a grimy head pops out of the tent. A man looks up at the new yogi and says thank you. In that moment he tells his life story, the broken promises, the fall from grace. It's all there in his eyes, a tragedy told in a single heartbeat.

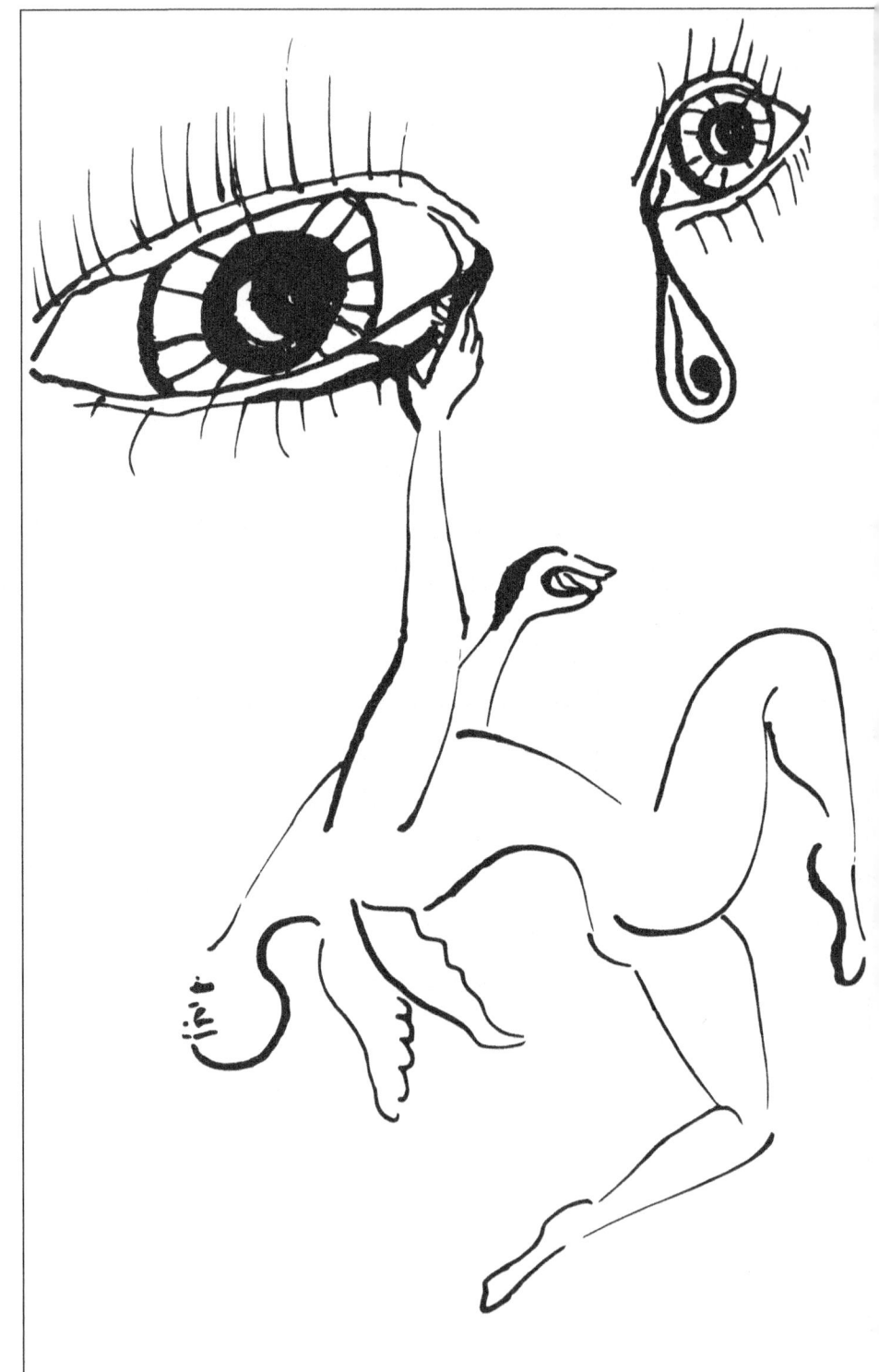

The new yogi stands there, her arms full of burritos. Her eyes convey a message back. The new yogi responds silently, energetically. What she says to him is this, "You told me your darkest secret. Now, tell me your brightest one. The beautiful brave thing you did that no one knows about. Come on, tell me."

These are the words of the new yogi.
They are being whispered all over the Earth.
They are being whispered in Ukraine. They
are being whispered in Nigeria.
Imagine a whisper incubating inside a cocoon.
Behold the chrysalis of a whisper, slowly
breaking out of its shell, slowly turning into
thunder, the thunder of Compassion, the
deafening roar of Integrity.

To all those peddlers of despair, to all those who flourish on cynicism, the new yogi looks them square in the eye and says, "I will not back down. I don't care about your statistics. I refuse to Big Picture myself into a coma. Whatever the effects of climate change, whatever the impact of greed on this planet, we will counteract it. I won't give in to doubt. I won't say yes to no for I believe that all that talent and courage and energy and perseverance and all those circuits and brain cells and mysteries and molecules and protons and electrons that call themselves Love will prevail, and this movement, this unstoppable forward progress gives me an unshakeable belief that humanity will be saved, and my fellow yogis and I will play an essential role in that great healing.

We will do it with joy in our
hearts, with style and grace, and with a bit of a
swagger, moving onward, dancing at the
speed of light, dancing at the speed of light,
dancing at the speed of light."

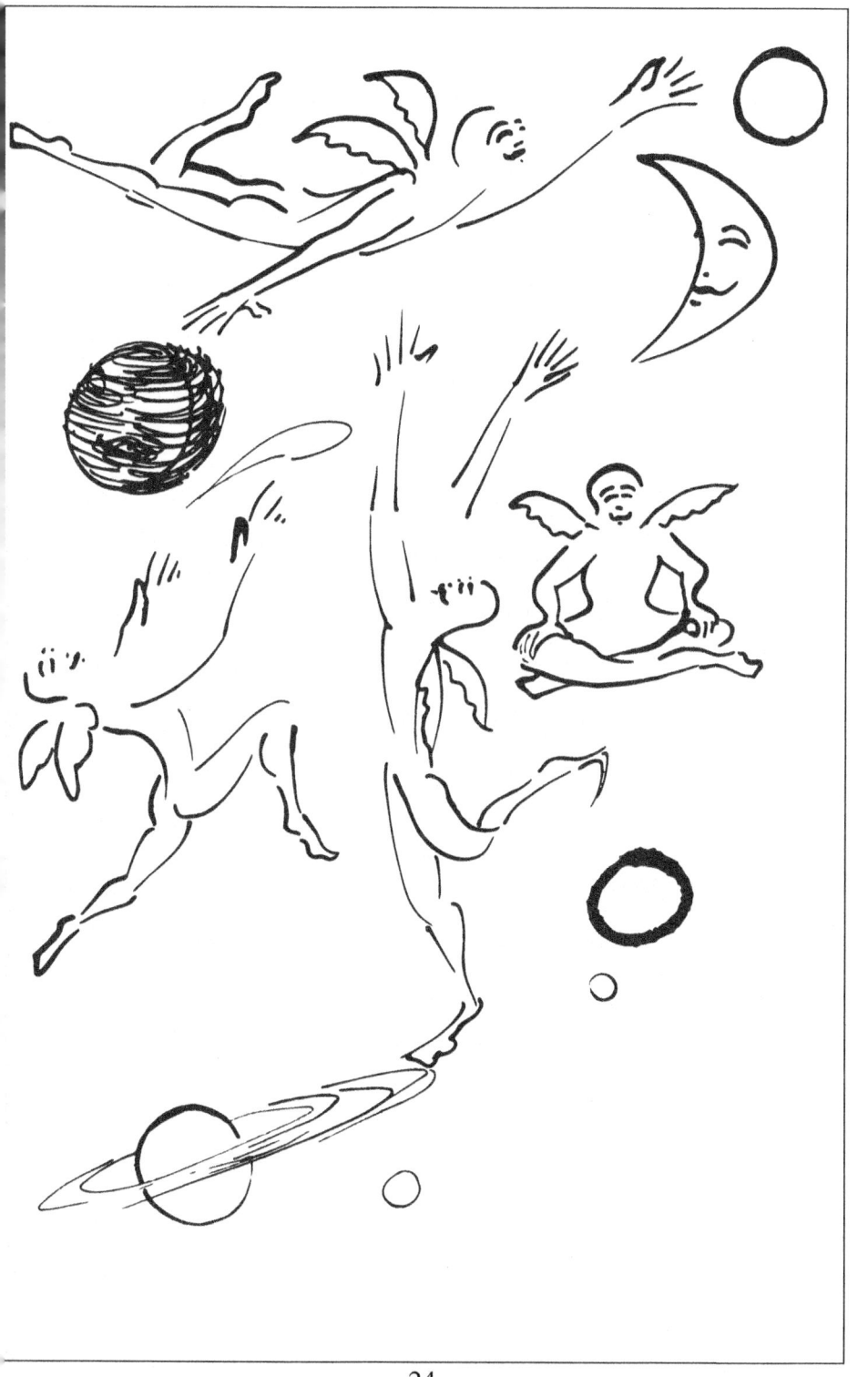

A Fairy's Guide To Riding Roses

First you must find a saddle
that fits between the thorns.
Do not try to mount a rose
with a shrunken heart.
It will buck you, kick you,
stomp on your lies.
If you end up on your back groaning
in the stable of blossoms,
keep one thing in mind,
never whip a flower.
Instead, feed your petal beast
a bale of wonder.

Then,

looping the leather reins

around its feral stem,

hoist yourself up and try again.

Just because you rode on a sunflower

across your kitchen table

doesn't mean you can gallop

across a field on the back of

a white rose. It takes practice.

If I were you I'd get started.

Some deserts can only be crossed
on the back of a rose.

Man with a Toolbox

Dawn broke.

Dawn was broken.

"What's going on?" asked Noon. "Why is it still dark out?"

"Dawn is broken," Morning moaned. "Midnight is to blame."

"Midnight, you are such a jerk," Noon screamed.

"Why is everyone always blaming me?" asked Midnight.

"Because you're always drunk."

"This may be true," said Midnight. "However, I did not break the dawn."

"If you didn't do it then who did?" asked Sunset.

"I think it was that last bomb," said Midnight. "It sure was a big one."

"Well what are we going to do?" Morning asked.

"Call a repair man,"
someone suggested.
That's exactly what they did.
A blue van pulled up outside
the front door of Midnight.
"Hello," said a man with a toolbox. "I
have come to repair the dawn."
"It's a rather unique line of work," said
Twilight. "How does one become a dawn
repair man?"
"Well," said the man, reaching for a hammer.
"I used to repair washing machines. But
every time I touched one it turned into a
hummingbird." He pulled a wrench out of his
toolbox. "I was watching an infomercial on
Christmas Eve. It talked about repairing really big
things. I decided to give it a shot."
He knelt down over Dawn.

A minute later, she rose in a flood of light.

"What happened?" Dawn said groggily.

"You were broken," explained Morning.

"I was?" Dawn said.

The repairman gathered up his tools.

"How much do we owe you?" asked Midnight.

"There's no charge."

"You mean you do all this for free?"

"I do it for the thrill. For the
simple pleasure of saying,
 'Hello, I have come to repair the dawn.'"

The Break-In

Love is breaking into my heart.
I barred the doors after I fell apart.
Love is fiddling with the latch.
Did I hear Love strike a match?
It doesn't matter. Nothing works on me.
Not even Love's master key.
But somehow Love is getting in.
My pain is growing very thin.
Down the hallway Love goes,
creeping on tiptoes.

Love Letter Written in Sears

Dear Antonina,
I'm sitting at a picnic table
in the lawn and garden section.
Three salesmen are watching me closely.
They're clustered together at the end of the aisle,
whispering nervously amongst themselves,
probably because I have a pen and notebook,
which means that I was sent
from the corporate headquarters to file a report.
They have no idea I'm writing a love letter.
Who'd ever write a love letter
on the third floor of Sears?
I'm the only one crazy enough to do that.
You're the only one crazy enough
to stick by the side of an unemployed cellist.
Don't worry.
Some day it will all pay off.
That prosperity meditation is working.
I can feel it.

Those poor salesmen.
They can't take their eyes off me,
especially the guy with thick glasses,
who hasn't sold a lawnmower in two weeks.
He is worried about getting laid off.
Whenever I glance up at him he flashes a big smile.
I wouldn't be surprised if he brings me a cup of coffee.
Or maybe even a donut.
After all, I'm the most powerful man in Sears.
And the most in love.

Taiwan

An air raid siren went off.
Mothers grabbed their children
off the swings and ran.
Traffic swerved, skidded, stopped.
People poured out of a bus into a supermarket.
The Taiwanese do this periodically
to prepare for an attack by Mainland China,
when and if it ever comes.
As I stood there,
something occurred to me.
If this was just a test
why was everyone freaking out?
Why were the ones who were by themselves
the most desperate to find shelter?
Maybe it was a different siren,
signaling a different kind of attack.
Maybe it was loneliness
launching another invasion.
I watched them running for their lives,
the German and French businessmen,
their wives thousands of miles away.
They scrambled into a school basement,
boarded up the windows.
I was the last remaining person
on the streets of Taipei.
I wasn't scared.
I had my love for you,
the deepest trench of all.
I dove into it.

A Lady Who Rides a Bike

It's hard not to like
a lady who rides a bike.
She doesn't even own a car.
Thinks Toyotas are so bizarre.
Down the boulevard coasting,
she smells better than coffee roasting.
In her basket a loaf of organic bread,
she laughs at what the wind just said.
So connected to the Earth,
she knows what a rose is worth.
Yellow flower in her hair.
All that beauty just isn't fair.
She hasn't touched meat since seventh grade,
believes in miracles, downdawg and fair trade.
Updown, downtown, wherever she goes,
she stays away from GMO's.

Pedaling past a palm tree,
with a hummingbird she jokes.
See how the setting sun
hits her silver spokes.
Gliding through gridlock,
she bids farewell to the angry faces.
She is off to kinder places.
She rings her little bell for me and waves.
To hold her in my arms is what my heart craves.
It's hard not to like
a lady who rides a bike.
Take it from me.
It's hard not to like
a lady who rides a bike.

Monarchs

How many glorious days do you plan on having? Days when you finally give yourself credit for all you've overcome, celebrating the smile that trekked the Himalayas to get to your face. A little smile and a coil of rope. Imagine it down by your shoelaces, a small bright thing ascending, over the ankle, along the thigh, climbing steadily, confidently, until suddenly it hears a wolf howling up ahead. Another answers.

A pair of regrets in the wilderness of your third chakra. Snow begins to fall. For the first time the smile becomes aware of all the forces arrayed against it, the wolves, the weather, the mountain itself, the incomparable vigor of all that is sad. The smile pushes on, hoisting itself onto your collarbone, dragging itself up over the crest of your chin, using every last muscle of brightness, planting its golden banner on your cheek, proclaiming to the world that you cannot be stopped.

How many glorious days do you plan on having? Quite a few, I suppose. All that meditation is weakening your weaknesses. Your despair is bedridden with the flu. Your ingratitude has laryngitis. Your anger got food poisoning after nibbling on compassion. It is marooned on a toilet seat. A glorious day indeed. In the stillness you catch a glimpse of all the remarkable things you're going to do with your life. In your deepest pasture you discover a herd of journeys, all of which raise their shaggy heads and stare at you. Every vein in each of their majestic bodies is a path that you will follow. A herd of journeys in a heart enraptured, a herd of journeys on a glorious day.

Today is just such a day. It begins with my girlfriend taking me to see the monarch migration. They spend the winter in a eucalyptus grove just north of Santa Barbara, fifty thousand butterflies swirling together in a gust of wind. I never knew that a single breeze could contain that much innocence.

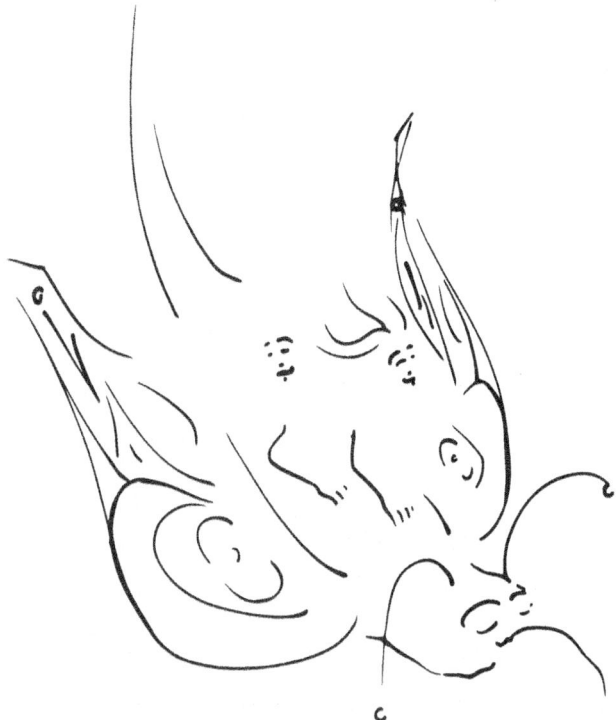

We stay for three hours. Who wouldn't want to linger in the gentlest place on Earth? Then we simply must go. If we stay one more minute we will overdose on astonishment.

We hop in the car and drive to Ojai for a New Year's Eve kirtan, three hundred people on a mountaintop chanting under the stars, lawyers, composers, architects, leaders in solar power, innovators in education, shrewd people with big hearts who are working on a cure for desolation, nothing flaky or narcissistic lurking beneath the tie-dye, chanting together, determined to pool our resources in the name of human decency, determined to infuse the next twelve months with some of the greatest moments in the history of healing. We honestly believe we can pull it off. And we are not drunk. There is too much hope flowing to worry about champagne.

We chant to forgive, to be forgiven.

We chant for Peace.

We are here to promote it, create it,
spread it, live it, be it, summon it,
declare it, embrace it, embody it,
proclaim it.

Peace.

At three in the morning, my true love and I drive back to Ventura to the house where she grew up. We are staying with her parents for the holidays. While she does some bedtime yoga stretches in the guest room upstairs, I go down into the kitchen for some almonds. Her mom and dad are sitting on a couch in the living room, watching a movie on TV about the hunt for Bin Laden. "They've finally found him," her mom whispers excitedly. "They're going in for the kill."

I move closer to the screen. I know I shouldn't. This
man may deserve to die but I do not need to revel in it.
I remember 9/11. The old desire for revenge caresses
me with its dirty fingers. I can feel the grace leaking
from my hatred. I am falling. It is a long drop from
butterflies to television. It doesn't take much
to ruin a glorious day. One thing is certain. If
I stay here and watch this, I will renounce
every vow I made on the mountaintop in Ojai. But I
can't peel my eyes off the screen. America will not be
safe until he is dead. How beautiful that lie is,
how impeccable in its treachery.

Far off in the distance I hear another chant,
"Death To Bin Laden, Death To Bin Laden."
It is being chanted in every big city, in every
small town, in every church, every temple.
It is being chanted by Democrats and Republicans.
I hear it in the Everglades, I hear
it on the prairie. Over that din I hear the voice
of my true love. She keeps yelling for me to
come to bed. We have to get up early and
drive down to LA for a Five Rhythms dance
that she has been looking forward to for
months.

Too bad.

I want to watch this bastard die. Men are
violent. We are full of rage. It will take us centuries to
climb out of that wheelchair. We don't have centuries.
I am aware of that. I am trying to evolve.
Why did the goddamn television have to be
on? I did not mean for this to happen. I came
here for almonds, a handful of almonds, not
vodka, not whiskey, almonds. I am innocent.
I haven't killed anyone. I've never even been
in a fistfight. I do volunteer work at a children's hospital.
Doesn't that mean something? All of creation
whispers in my ear, "It is not enough."

Well, it's too late. The marines have searched the compound. There's only one room left.

Bin Laden is inside that room, fast asleep. The soldiers are so graceful in their deadliness they do not wake him up. Silently stealthily, they plant an explosive on the door. It blows open. They burst into the room, raise their M16's. Before they can pull their triggers, before they can fire off a round, I am being dragged out of the room by my girlfriend. She is clutching me with her lovely little fingers. This slender woman half my size almost lifts me off the ground, oblivious to the television, to what is going on inside my head. She just wants to shake her booty on New Year's Day and she knows what she has to do. She yanks me upstairs into the bedroom. I do not resist. She slams the door shut, looks me square in the eye and says,
"We are going to bed right now."

That is when you know that you're in a good relationship.

It Doesn't Get Much Better Than This

I was doing yoga in a cemetery.
Along came three wild turkeys.

Love Swept the Floor

Love swept the floor.

The floor turned into a window.
It thanked Love. "I always wanted
to be a window."

A man entered the room, frowning.

"No floor? How am I
supposed to get to the other side?"
"Walk on me," said Love.
The man took a tentative step.
He took another step.
He walked on Love
for one thousand years.

He became a door.
Through the creaking of
his hinges, he whispered,
"I wish I was a window."

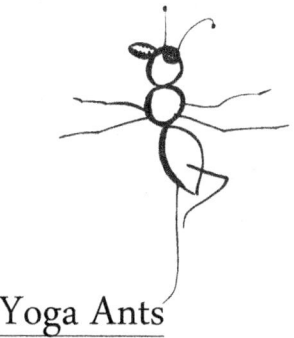

Yoga Ants

I unrolled my yoga mat on the end of the dock. I've always done yoga in dark crowded sweaty urban spaces. Never outside. Never like this. I couldn't believe how beautiful it was, a smile made out of pelicans, the sun fastening a ray of light around a seagull's leg. The hungry bird delivered the golden note. The merciful mind of the lake was busy dividing the day into breezes. Then along came the ant. Have you ever tried to meditate with something crawling up your arm? I flicked him onto the dock. Undeterred, he marched up my left ankle. I brushed him off.

He came back. He kept coming back,
a black dot, a period appearing abruptly
in the middle of a serene sentence,
prematurely ending my paragraph
of peace and quiet. The chapter of
my enlightenment ruined.
Time for drastic action.
I scooped him onto my key chain and
banished him to the other end of the dock.
Five minutes later, he scuttled across my mat
lugging a dead caterpillar. There I was, trying
to be non-violent, and he's out there
slaughtering caterpillars. Bringing Death onto
my yoga mat. At this point, I felt the need to
speak directly to the ant.

"You little bastard. Can't you see I need to relax? You have no idea the pressure I'm under. My girlfriend just left me. I've got problems. I've got serious emotional problems." At this point, the ant felt the need to respond. "Emotional problems? What the hell is an emotional problem? My life is simple. I search. I forage. I'm tireless. I'm committed. My dedication to my fellow ants is absolute." I had to give the critter credit. He certainly was focused and did live in harmony with the other periods in nature's dictionary. And it was hard not to marvel at his strength. I decided to let him crawl up my arm. I would not resist.

He motored all the way to my chin, crept down a passageway on the side of my head, not my ear canal, a different path. I felt him exploring my interior. He emerged, carrying something gigantic and rancid, my anger. He dragged it down my arm onto the dock and squeezed it into a crack in the concrete, then he came back and dragged off my self-pity, my resentment, my pettiness, a tiny tireless creature plunging again and again into my center, taking things out, until there was nothing left except the universe.

Scales

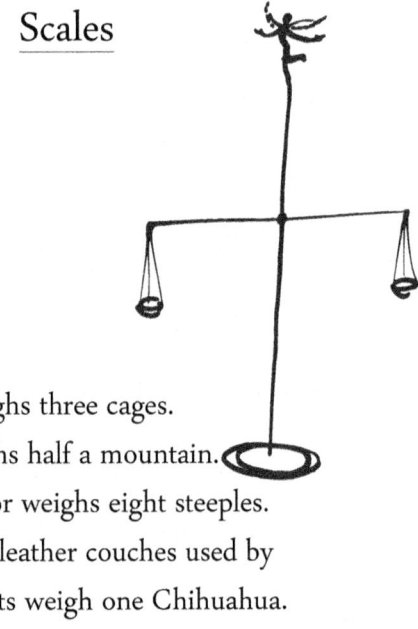

One sneer weighs three cages.
Half a lie weighs half a mountain.
One dance floor weighs eight steeples.
One thousand leather couches used by
psychotherapists weigh one Chihuahua.

Finally I Can Relax

Sprawled out in a claw footed tub,
listening to a blue jay in the
apricot tree outside the foggy
window, I began to wonder
if I myself was a kind of tub,
shaped like a human being.
God was sprawled out inside me,
soaking in the blood.

Love Thing

"What is music?"

"Love."

"What is dancing?"

"Love."

"Explain quantum physics."

"Love."

"Tell me about homeless people."

"Love.

"What's the best thing that ever happened to you?"

"Love."

"What's the second best thing that ever happened to you?"

"Love."

"What's your favorite pizza topping?"

"Love."

"Where do you come from?"

"Love."

"Where are you going?"

"Love."

"Why aren't you bitter?"

"Love."

"Why aren't you on anti-depressants?"

"Love."

"What is yoga?"

"Love."

"What is meditation?"

"Love."

"What do you think of Muslims?"

"Love."

"Tell me about North Korea."

"Love."

"The dictionary of heaven is one word long. What is that word?"

"Love."

"What does the wind call you?"

"Love."

"Tell me about your grandmother."

"Love."

"What is your foundation?"

"Love."

"What's the holiest thing you ever did?"

"Love."

"What is bigger than a swastika?"

"Love."

"Tell me about all the people who piss you off."

"Love."

"What about all those who betrayed you?"

"Love."

"What about the ones who gossip behind your back?"

"Love."

"What's another name for strength?"

"Love."

"What's another name for true power?"

"Love."

"Who was Martin Luther King Jr.?"

"Love."

"Who's most in favor of gay marriage?"

"Love."

"Tell me about hummingbirds."

"Love."

"What's another name for a tree frog?"

"Love."

"What's that hop in your step?"

"Love."

"What's that light in your eyes?"

"Love."

"How do you know all this?"

"Love."

"How can you be so certain?"

"Love.

"What the hell is going on here?"

"Love."

"Then what happened?"

"Love."

"What's two plus two?"

"Love."

"What's seven billion plus one?"

"Love."

"What's the only thing you'd ever take over a red velvet cupcake?"

"Love."

"What is the secret of your success?"

"Love."

"Who defeated Stalin?"

"Love."

"Who abolished slavery?"

"Love."

"Who gave women the right to vote?"

"Love."

"How will we bring about peace in the Middle East?"

"Love."

"What's it like to be with your family on Thanksgiving?"

"Love."

"Tell me about your mother."

"Love."

"Tell me about your father."

"Love."

"What kind of work do you do?"

"Love."

"Where did you go to school?"

"Love."

"What do you have a degree in?"

"Love."

"Tell me about all the mistakes you ever made."

"Love."

"What is evolution?"

"Love."

"What is the present moment?"

"Love."

"Who will you be 1000 years from now?"

"Love."

"What is your master plan?"

"Love."

"What is the last word in this poem, the only word we could possibly end on, the only word that has any meaning in the universe, the one word that will endure, that is deathless. What is that word?"

"Love."

"One more for the road."

"Love."

"I lied. That wasn't the last time. This is the last time. Let's hear it one last time."

"Love."

"Again."

"Love."

"Softer this time."

"Love."

"A whisper."

"Love."

"Another whisper."

"Love."

"The final whisper, the one that will go around the world."

"Love."

The Drought

It takes three hundred years without any rain
to produce a Nazi. A racial slur
can only be spoken through parched lips
dying for a sip of water. A kid who marches
into a cafeteria with a shotgun and opens fire
has never even seen a drop of rain.
We are that thirsty.

The greed on Wall Street only exists because
the water coolers are empty. All across America
faucets don't work. I know a woman who spent
her 20's standing under a shower nozzle, trying
to wash off her childhood. She couldn't get clean.
None of us can. Layers of dirt keep piling up
on our species. 64,000 homeless children
in Los Angeles County. We can't escape that fact.
Nowhere to go, not even a bookstore.
Words don't drip anymore. They used to drip
all the way down to the bottom of the soul.
You can try all you want. There ain't much
moisture in a text message.

Where can we turn? Entire religions are dehydrated.
Who is to blame for the drought? We all are.
Each one of us added a crack to the dry riverbed
of the human heart. As we sit there, being honest
with ourselves, there is the rumor of a storm
approaching. Some clouds have been sighted,
a vast weather system, tropical, Aquarian,
heading in our direction.

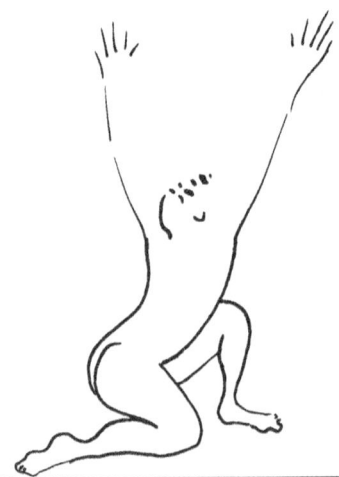

Big gray clouds slide in front of the scorching sun. A gorgeous gloom settles over the city. Clouds dance in majestic slow motion. We look up, mesmerized by the choreography. A six year old girl opens her mouth and sticks out her tongue. The first drop lands precisely on the tip of her tongue. She tastes it. It tastes her,

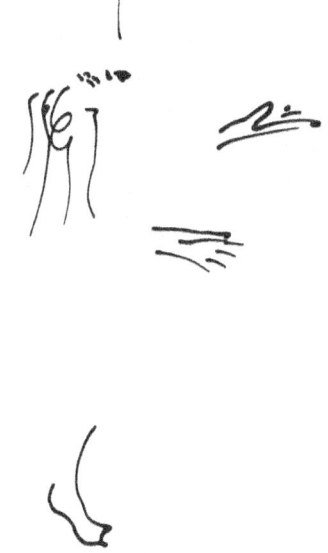

a drop of rain tasting a little girl, her hope, her wonder, her imagination. Delicious.
This is a species worth saving. A second drop falls, then a third, and another and another. Then it stops. The dark clouds don't dissolve or disband or drift away nor do they unload their precious cargo. The tropical storm produces ten drops of rain.

Whoever heard of a ten drop tempest? What a tease.
What a torture. What the hell is going on?
Is this just some New Age hoax? Just some
phony spirituality? A light drizzle of the soul?
Some of us wonder if it was our fault, our
generation, a generation that lacked the grit
required to do the hard work. We didn't want
to be disturbed by human suffering. We weren't
in the mood for the hassle. We'd rather sit in
a vegan café and sip a twelve dollar smoothie.
We had too many gadgets in our hands to
take hold of Life. We were too busy. We
couldn't find the time to be extraordinary.
No, we couldn't find the time to be extraordinary.
Is that all this is? Is that all that we've created?
Is that all this amounts to? Ten drops of rain?

The mother of the little girl whose tongue got rained on drags her daughter kicking and screaming back into the house. Others follow. They give up. They go back to the television. A few remain. We breathe. We meditate. We go deeper into our practice. The air does not reek of pot smoke. No one is dropping acid. We seek no escape from the truth. We are disciplined, determined, focused, non-reactive.

We are patient.

Patient.

Patient.

A drop of rain splatters on a yoga mat.

Then the storm begins.

Nothing has ever fallen from the sky quite
like this, subtle and relentless. This is no hoax.
The commitment is real, the courage is real,
the vision is real, the service is real, the teachings
are real, the technology is real, the movement
is real. It is scary. Frantically we pile sandbags
around our egos to protect our small way of thinking.
The rain rips right through them. It smashes
through our umbrellas, through our foul weather
gear, into our pores, penetrating deeper and
deeper, through flesh and bone, to a
golden place on the other side of marrow.

Have you ever smelled a species waking up?
Have you ever caught a whiff of that scent?
Point your nose directly at your essence.
Inhale the freshness of rain-soaked pine,
cedar, wild mint, the little forest dripping in
your center. No stench can withstand the fury
of that immortal fragrance.

The rain is falling. It will not stop. The levee breaks.
Corporations get flooded. From the hardest
hit there comes a ray of light called immaculate
leadership. Pranayam is practiced in boardrooms,
in high schools. On a Wednesday morning
at 9:23am, the last gas station in America
serves its last gallon of gas to the last automobile
that runs on fossil fuel. Later that night, at four
in the morning, in the heart of a big city, a
woman rides the subway by herself without
a trace of fear.

The rain grows fiercer. It is so heavy and so mysterious it seeps down and down, through holes and cracks and conduits, the merest of passageways, into the spirit world. A puddle spreads into the afterlife, soaking our ancestors with the revelation that no one died in vain.

All that hardship and sacrifice was not for nothing and this cannot be ignored or denied or repudiated because finally, at the end of history's long stem, there blooms a flower of compassion.

Behold a waterfall cascading from an act of mercy. Behold your inner strength, a wild animal called Brightness.

Behold the crumbling empire, empire
of despair, empire of violence, the pillars of hatred
and racism caving in, the foundation buckling.

We have reached the tipping point.

Torrential rain forms great lakes of higher
consciousness. Way out in the middle, miles
from shore, something floats to the surface,
something that has been lost since the beginning
of time, the crown of stillness, the only true crown,
a crown so big it can be worn by all of humanity,
one crown on all heads. It rises up from the depths
for the poor, the rich, the powerful,
the powerless. Seven billion kings and queens sharing
the crown of stillness, the grand and glorious crown
of our species, discarded by ignorance, recovered
by the storm, scrubbed clean by the pouring rain.

It sparkles with inner peace. It gleams
with humility and compassion. It fits
your head perfectly. Oh how good it feels to
be regal, to not be shackled by a single ounce
of pride, to no longer crave approval or
recognition, to no longer be in the grip of fear,
to have finally defeated jealousy and pettiness,
to have forgotten your story. Enthroned in the
present moment in the middle of a yoga class,
listening to a choir of silences. No one says a word.
You let the silence break the silence.
Oh how beautiful you are.
Never has there been such beauty
in the world as a group of people waking up
to their true nature, no longer separate,
putting on the crown together,
the crown of stillness.
Your crown on your head
in this moment forever.

At the end of class, you place your forehead on your mat and peer down into the well. You fill your canteen with laughter and your jug with grace. No one will leave your presence thirsty. You will wander the face of the Earth in the pouring rain, the rain that will not let up, the rain that is unceasing. 50 million people doing yoga, 200 million, 800 million.

As the storm intensifies
and becomes even more passionate,
a phoenix rises into the night sky,

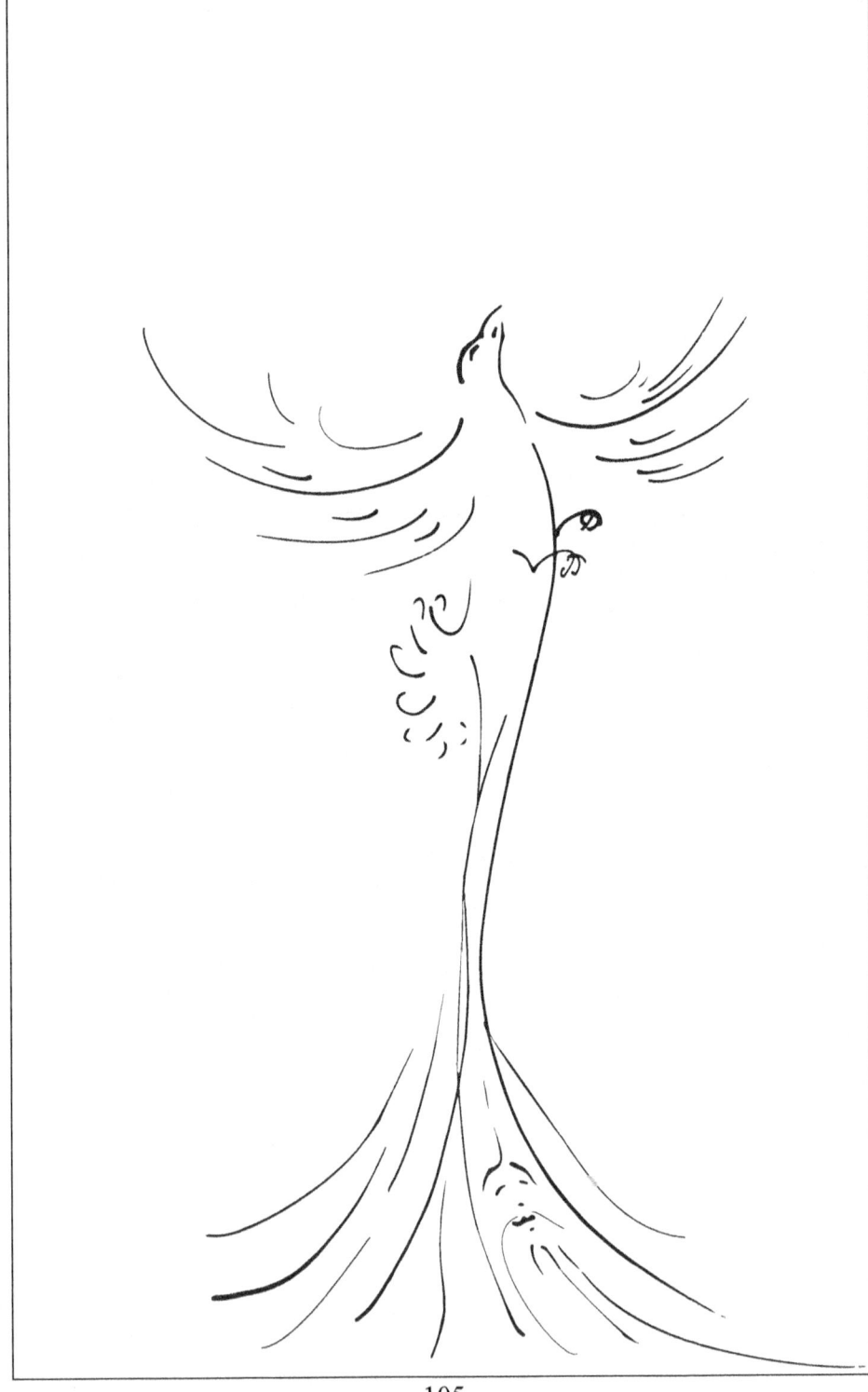

with wet wings and a
thundering melody,
singing your song, our song,
one song, proclaiming,

"It is over.
The drought is over!"

Acknowledgments

James and Oshri would like to thank Yoga West and the entire teacher training team, along with their fellow graduates. We would also like to thank Guru Singh, Adarsh Khalsa, Amrit Singh, and Kewal Kaur for your friendship, your commitment to your students, and your devotion to sharing the teachings. We would also like to give special thanks to Mary Harper, Jagatpal Singh, Fatehbir Kaur, Dhanpal Quesada, Harprem Jeet, Kuljeet, Claudia Stewart Navarro, and Camilla D'Avignon for helping to make Yoga West what it is.

James Mihaley would also like to thank James Price, Rick Adams, Jim Miller, Yuval Ron and Philip Holahan for their extraordinary support. James would also like to thank his dear friends Jared Cyr, Claire Austin, Jo Cobett, Marlene Sway, Mike & Donna Pedraza, Jacquie & Ravi from Khalsa Peace Corps, Bill and Betty Parsons, Jamie & Daniel Alcheh, and Rick Harabes.

Oshri would also like to thank Ahmad Jitan, Alex Modestou and Katharine Eggleston, Amy Serwitz, Andrew and Krista Wang, Anya Belkina, Augustine Senesie, Bhumi Purohit, Carol Shih, Cheryl Kline, Chris McGuire and Allison Barker, Chuck Abolt, Cosette Wong, Daniel Lockman, David Shapiro, Diana Hufford, Dohnbi Kim, Efrem Harkham, Gabriella Garcia-Pardo, Gale Stafford, Grecco Buratto, Harinam Singh, Hari Shankar, Hayk Makhmuryan, Hilda Lopez, Isaac Bangura, Isabelle Figaro, Jai Inder Singh, Jamie Patrick, Jessica Enman, Joseph Robinson, Joshua Reitzenstein, Julia Romanskaya, Julia Tyler, Keith Ferrazzi, Lokesh Anand, Lynn Rosen, Mahankirn Khalsa, Marissa Bergmann, Maryam Shabazz, Mashal Saif, Meg Williams, Michael and Elizabeth Federman, Mohamed Pa-Momo Fofanah, Natan Halevy, Paul Sherman, Rachel and Daniel Hughes, Rachel Shorr, Rachel White, Rajasree Roy, Ramdas Menon, Richard and Cindy Lucas, Richard Rosenblatt, Roxanna and Rebbeca Goudarzi, Saffa Damba, Sean Bennett, Sean Rosario, Sunshine Best, Tannu Kaur, Tawd Dorenfeld, Teru and Jan, The Simons, The Grabels, Tony Ocean, Ustad Bismillah Khan Sahib-Ji, Warren Rustand, Yoknyam Dabale, Youmna Sherif, Ziggy Yoediono for your friendship, mentorship, teachings, love, and vibes.

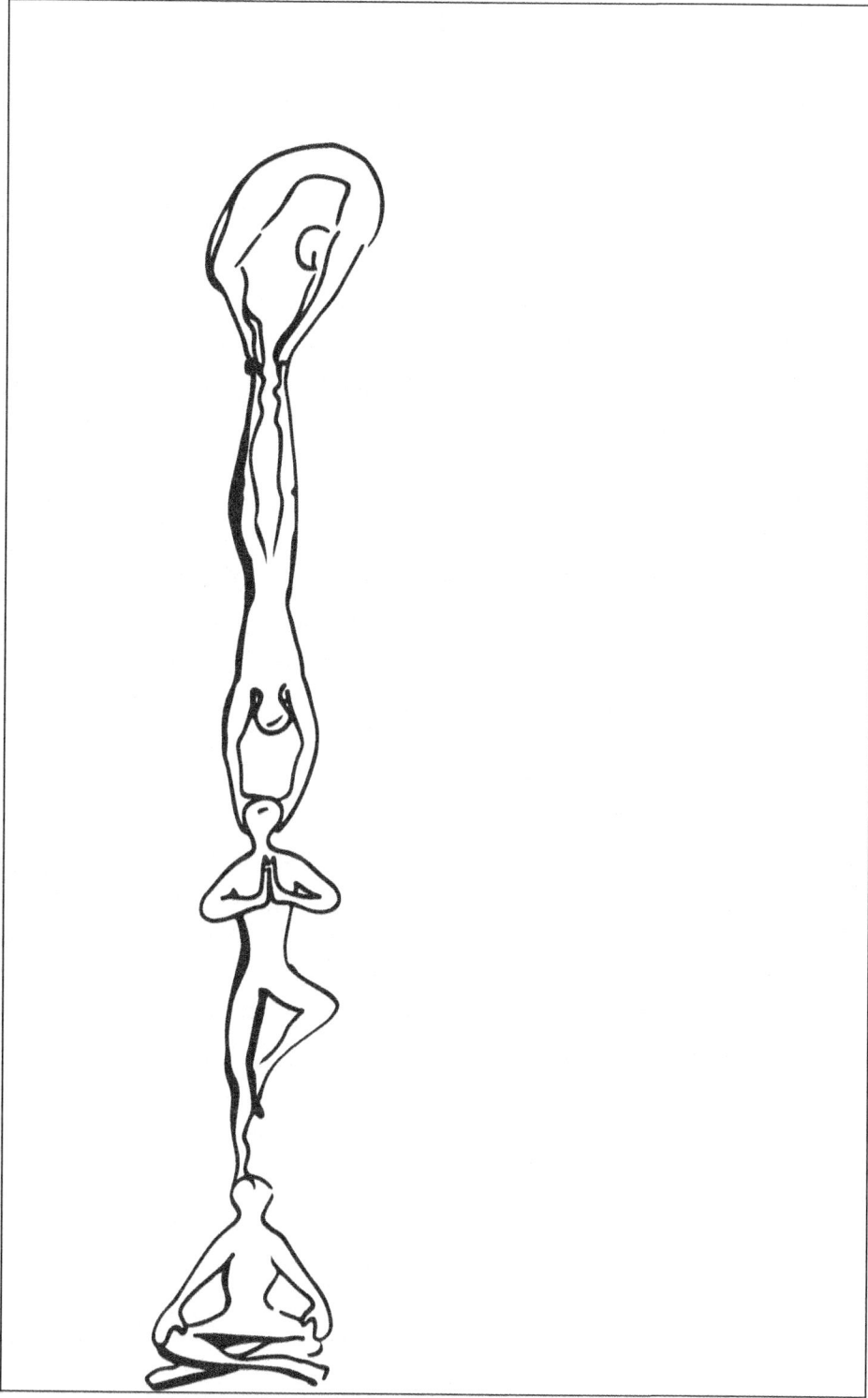

About the Artists

James Mihaley found peace of mind in Los Angeles by doing volunteer work for five years at a children's hospital. He also found it in a food truck, rolling burritos on Skid Row. James eats more kale than anyone in America. He likes to walk in the moonlight. He is a nocturnal pedestrian. He loves to do live performances of this poetry collection. To book James for a spoken word event please contact: Jmihaley@yahoo.com Or call: 323-620-0832

Oshri Hakak is thankful to have art and music created through him for uplifting as much as possible. He's also a beekeeper and a Babylonian Jew and a Human Being. He's a fan of babies and particularly likes bounding about with his bubbling nieces, Elah and Noa, and his beautiful nephew, Aiden. More of his art can be viewed on www.LivingInkFlow.com, where there's also a place to sign up to receive the daily ink he sends out every morning for you.

To find out more about The New Yogi Manifesto, order posters of the artwork, or get in touch with the artists, please go to: *www.newyogi.yoga*

Chariot of Kindness, publisher of beautiful books

CPSIA information can be obtained at www.ICGtesting.com
Printed in the USA
BVOW07s1937030615

403124BV00003B/7/P